M000101377

Embracing Our Priestly Nature at Work

A theology and practice for ordinary saints

Scott Breslin

RESOURCE *Publications* · Eugene, Oregon

EMBRACING OUR PRIESTLY NATURE AT WORK
A Theology and Practice for Ordinary Saints

Copyright © 2017 Scott Breslin. All rights reserved. Except for brief quotations in critical publications or reviews, no part of this book may be reproduced in any manner without prior written permission from the publisher. Write: Permissions, Wipf and Stock Publishers, 199 W. 8th Ave., Suite 3, Eugene, OR 97401.

Resource Publications
An Imprint of Wipf and Stock Publishers
199 W. 8th Ave., Suite 3
Eugene, OR 97401

www.wipfandstock.com

PAPERBACK ISBN: 978-1-5326-3670-7
HARDCOVER ISBN: 978-1-5326-3672-1
EBOOK ISBN: 978-1-5326-3671-4

Manufactured in the U.S.A.   09/25/17

Art work: Jeanette Engqvist

Layout: Alice Hägg

Title Page: If you study the mirrored reflection of the construction worker, chef and nurse, you may discover the self-identity that this booklet is attempting awaken and invoke.

All Scripture comes from the NIV (1984) unless otherwise noted.

Testimonials

It not only helps me understand my identity in Christ in a secular world, it also gives me the healthy perspective to declare - to proclaim, as Scott puts it - the praises of God in my everyday existence. **Lawrence Tong, International Director of OM**

Breslin has been multiplying his life throughout the Middle East and North Africa for 30 years! Take him seriously. This book, which when applied could cause the reader to find a hugely satisfying lifestyle significantly beyond the "God doesn't use me" assumptions s/he previously held. This deeply thought-provoking work should stimulate many to embrace their priestly identity at work. **Dr. Greg Livingstone, Founder, Frontiers**

This book packs a powerful wallop. It may be small, but the ideas and proposal it outlines are HUGE. Scott explains and explores what happens when followers of Jesus understand and embrace the call to be "priests" in the places where we work and live. And he is absolutely right – this is the stuff or radical transformation. I heartily recommend this great new resource for churches and small groups. **Steven Bradbury, Director of the Micah 6:8 Centre, Eastern College Australia and former National Director of TEAR Australia (1984-2009)**

Across the Church today, few issues are more urgent and essential than the need to rediscover our vocation as the royal priesthood of all believers. As such, we are called to participate in God's mission of reconciliation in every sphere of life - in work and school, in gym and shop, in field and factory, Monday to Saturday, as well as in gathered church on Sunday. This study is a thoroughly grounded, very practical introduction to our priestly vocation – equipping us to participate fully in God's mission in the world, and embrace the transformational role we are each called to play in our workplaces. **Matthew Frost, Chief Executive, Tearfund UK (2005-2015)**

With clarity, wisdom and grace, Scott plumbs the depths of this critical area and offers the reader a variety of practical handles on how to fulfill your priestly role in the modern marketplace. I heartily recommend this invaluable resource for both individual and small group study. You will be blessed by it and want to pass it on to others. **Rev. Dr. Daniel Meyer, Senior Pastor, Christ Church of Oak Brook, Illinois. Yale, BA, Princeton Seminary, MDiv, Fuller Seminary, DMin**

It is said that "A picture is worth a thousand words". This book will paint a picture that will add strength to your self-identity, leading to purpose and fulfillment in your own life while becoming a blessing in your workplace. **Jan Sturesson, Chairman of the International Christian Chamber of Commerce**

Thought provoking! Scott's exposition of the idea of priestly responsibility in the work place helped me to go deeper in my thinking about how to integrate my faith and scientific career. I especially appreciated his emphasis on blessing others, a topic often ignored. As a marine biologist, the next challenge is for me is to think about how to apply these ideas and his PRIEST model to the ocean itself. **Dr. Robert Sluka, Ph.D., Marine and Coastal Conservation Programme, A Rocha International**

About the Author

 Dr. Scott Breslin is the International Director of Operation Mercy, an international relief & development NGO based in Sweden. He has worked as a training and management consultant for PwC (PricewaterhouseCoopers), Honeywell Corporation, Nordic School of Management, and other multinational organizations in Europe, Central Asia, Middle East, and N. America. He holds an MSc in Business Education and a M.Div. in Counselling. Scott's doctorate in education is from the University of Edinburgh. Scott is married to Katarina and the father of four adult children.

Contents

Chapter 1

Introduction

At the core of every follower of Jesus exists a priestly DNA, designed by God to be a prominent part of our nature. However, like a slow burning ember, this priestly identity risks remaining obscure and inconsequential unless fanned to life. This book was designed to help facilitate the process of making our priestly identity more prominent in our lives, particularly our work lives a. It is the result of observation, research, reflection, and nearly four decades of practice in workplaces in North America, Europe, Asia and the Middle East. All of which have reinforced to me the importance of embracing a core self-identity that is consistent, sustainable and biblical.

In the following chapters, I construct a definition of what it means to be a priestly people and suggest how we can practically live out our priestly identity in real life, especially life at work. The biblical meanings of our priestly nature may surprise you. You may be happy to know that it has nothing to do with wearing creepy black clothes, lighting incense, or hanging out in church buildings. To discover the real meanings of our priestly nature we need to take a fresh look at the Bible and be willing to realign our thinking with what we find. Centuries before Martin Luther and other Reformation leaders began promoting the concept we know today as the universal priesthood or priesthood of all believers, Moses (Exodus 19:5-6), Peter (1 Peter 2:5-9), and John (Rev. 5:10, 20:6) had already been teaching it. This doctrine is not the sole domain of Protestants. The Roman Catholic Church[1] and other Christian traditions make allowance for this doctrine. While not a new concept, for some reason the priesthood of all believers has remained an abstract doctrine instead of an integral dimension of our self-identity. As such, most of us rarely think of ourselves as a priest. This needs to change because God had something important in mind when he designed his people to be his priests. Our priesthood is not a metaphor, but a real God-given role identity. If we embrace it as core to who we are, we can expect our attitudes and behaviors to change. Yet, embracing a priestly self-identity is not without obstacles. It requires us to navigate past our own culturally derived misunderstandings of what it means to

---

[1] For example, Vatican II discusses this subject in its "Decree on the Apostolate of the Laity." Also see paragraphs 1546 of the Catechism of the Catholic Church (1994).

be a priest and to adopt meanings that are consistent with the biblical narrative. It also requires us to embrace a self-identity that will not likely be reinforced by fellow Christians unless we radically reinvent the status quo. However, if we manage to make this cognitive journey, we will find ourselves in a much better position to represent Jesus to our families, communities, and work colleagues. Embracing our priestly self-identity should be radically transformational.

In the following chapters, I will argue that embedded in the biblical meaning of priest is the idea of being sent or appointed to represent, and it carries with it authority and responsibility. Like two sides of a coin, priests represent God to their people and represent their people to God. The universal priesthood is a type of agency entrusted to all followers of Jesus. While only some followers of Jesus are gifted apostles (sent ones), all followers of Jesus are indeed sent to represent as a consequence of their God-given priestly identity.

The Bible mentions a handful of God-given role identities bestowed on all followers of Jesus. These include: child of God, saint, servant, disciple, friend, ambassador and priest. Interestingly, the meanings of these God-given role identities are rarely explicitly defined in the Scriptures. Bible study, research, reflection, and discussion are needed to reshape our understanding. Otherwise, by default, our understanding of these role identities will continue to be largely molded by our cultural and social contexts rather than informed and shaped by the Bible.

In the following chapters we will see how Scripture can help us delineate what aspects of following Jesus are particularly priestly, and teach us how these priestly duties can be practiced in the workplace, no matter what our context. We will discuss how our priestly nature is not dependent on our occupation, spiritual gifts, personality, ethnicity, gender or education, but these and other things will shape how our priesthood is expressed. I argue that the workplace is one of the primary contexts where God calls his followers to fulfill the Great Commission of Matthew 28:19-20. For most of us, the secular workplace will be our parish, and our work colleagues and clients will be our parishioners. Plain and simple, the workplace is the primary "mission field" God ordains for most adults.

As such, our priesthood is meant to be integral to our self-identity and more fundamental to who we are than our occupational identity, ethnic identity, or nationality. While all our God-given role identities are important, in the following chapters, I argue there is something especially important and missional about our priestly identity. It is as if our priestly nature is a summation of our child, servant, saint, friend and ambassadorial role identities.

Suggestions on How to Use this Book

This booklet will likely have greater impact if it is used as part of a small group study. In my experience, developing and sustaining a priestly self-identity requires being part of a community of like-minded followers of Jesus who help reinforce it. If you are not already part of a community of people who purpose to follow Jesus, join one or form one as soon as possible.

Over a dozen small groups have been experimenting with different ways to use this booklet in group settings. Here are some of the ideas they have generated.

- Since there are ten chapters, a small group might do one chapter a session. Each chapter is 3-5 pages followed by five discussion questions.
- Some groups recommended reading chapters aloud during the small group sessions. It takes an average of 5-10 minutes to read one chapter aloud.
- Some groups found it helpful for each member to read the whole booklet at least once before going through the booklet chapter by chapter as a group.
- Some groups recommended that each group member read the chapter at home so that during the group session more time could be invested in looking up the Bible references and discussing the questions.

- Most group leaders created additional discussion questions.

Others are using this study in one-on-one mentoring. However you use this material, there will be added value if you can discuss it with others. As my mother use to say, "Nothing worth doing well is worth doing alone."

Questions for Reflection:

1. While these verses will come up again later, look up the following verses and discuss what they mean. Exodus 19:5-6, 1 Peter 2:5-9, and Revelation 5:10, 20:6.
2. When you hear the word "priest" what comes to mind? Is it a negative image or a positive image? Please explain.
3. How might this study help reduce any negative images or mental obstacles you have, if any, in regard to embracing a priestly self-identity?
4. What is the mirrored reflection of the construction worker, chef and nurse (see front cover) trying to communicate?
5. What approach will your group use to go through this study?

Chapter 2
The Universal Priesthood of Believers

In the Old Testament, the Levites were set apart to serve as priests to the people of Israel. Yet, it is sometimes overlooked that all of Israel (not just the Levites) were meant to be priests. Consider what God says to the people of Israel through Moses in Exodus 19:5-6 (emphasis added):

> Now if you obey me fully and keep my covenant, then out of all nations you will be my treasured possession. Although the whole earth is mine, *you will be for me a kingdom of priests* and a holy nation. These are the words you are to speak to the Israelites.

Here we see that the concept of the priesthood of all believers can be traced to the days of Moses and Exodus 19, and not just to Martin Luther and other Reformation leaders. The whole nation of Israel was to serve as a kingdom of priests. In fact, it was not until Exodus 28 (nine chapters later) that the Levitical priesthood was established. It seems that members of the Levitical priesthood were to be priests to the priests, so to speak. Thus, in the Old Testament we find there are two streams, or orders, of priests set apart by God. The first being the priesthood of all God's people and the second being the Levitical priesthood. However, with the death and resurrection of Jesus, Hebrews chapters 7-10 indicates that the temporal era of the Levitical priesthood came to a close while the universal priesthood of all believers continues, with Jesus as the high priest.

In the New Testament, all of God's people continue to be called priests. For example in 1 Peter 2:5 and 2:9, writing to both Jewish and Gentile followers of Jesus, Peter says:

> ... you also, like living stones, are being built into a spiritual house to be a holy priesthood...
>
> ... you are a chosen people, a royal priesthood, a holy nation, a people belonging to God...

The doctrine of the priesthood of all believers continues from the Old Testament to the New Testament. Unlike the Old Testament era, there are not two streams or orders of priests, but rather different gifts and roles within one order. Perhaps a functional equivalent of the dual priesthood model of the Old Testament is reflected in Ephesians 4:11-13. Here we see that people gifted as apostles, prophets, evangelists, pastors, and teachers are given the task to "prepare God's people for works of service." After all, the Levitical priests, in part, also helped prepare God's people (the Israelites) for works of service. However, it is a bit of a stretch (and theologically unnecessary) to endow higher priestly credentials to apostles, prophets, evangelists, pastors and teachers than have already been allotted them by virtue of their membership in God's family.

Whether our Christian tradition makes a distinction between laity and clergy is not particularly significant in this discussion. What is relevant is even if we belong to a Christian tradition that makes a distinction between laity and clergy those of us who are "laity" still have a priestly identity even if it is not a formal office within our church tradition. The "laity" are the bi-vocational segment of the Church in that we hold both the office/nature of a priest, as well as the occupational, where we live out our calling and earn our living.

Our Priestly Core

Here is one way to look at it: at our core exists a priestly God-given identity. All followers of Jesus hold this in common. However, our SHAPE[2] (Spiritual Gifts, Heart, Ability, Personality, and Experience) makes us different and unique from one another.

The combination of being both the same and different simultaneously fosters community. The "sameness" gives us unity

---

[2] See Rick Warren's book, The Purpose Driven Life, Zondervan, 1997

of purpose, while being "different" promotes interdependence. Our priestly nature is at the core of who we are. Our SHAPE strongly influences how our priestly nature is expressed, just as the thickness and nature of the layers of a ball, as well as the surface (context), will affect the way a ball will bounce. Of course, our self-identity is much more complex than this analogy, but it illustrates how our God-given priestly nature is core to our identity. It also reflects why there will be countless variations of how our priestly natures will be expressed depending on our SHAPE and context.

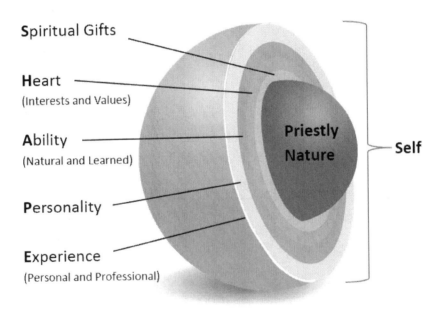

When we consider Galatians 3:28, we discover that gender, race and social positon are not part of the criteria for the priestly order envisioned in Exodus 19:6 and 1 Peter 2:9. Peace with God seems to be the primary criteria for membership in this priestly order.

Peace with God can only be found in Jesus Christ. Therefore, whether we are laity or clergy, male or female, slave or free, Jew or gentile, young or old, Catholic or Protestant, all followers of Jesus have a God-given role identity as priests.

The Eternal Nature of Our Priesthood

According to Hebrews 7, Jesus became God's complete and final peace-offering for mankind, and the era of the Levitical priesthood and the role of the temple was brought to a close. After the destruction of the temple in 70 AD, the Levitical priesthood stopped playing a role even in Judaism. However, the priestly nature and mission of God's people continues with even greater clarity. Hebrews 7 and 8 reveals that Jesus is our High Priest, but not a high priest of the Levitical order. Instead, followers of Jesus are aligned under Jesus in the ancient priestly order of Melchizedek (Hebrews 7:10-17). We will talk a bit more about Melchizedek later. The point I want to make here is the priestly order of Melchizedek predates the Levitical priesthood and Israel. While the Levitical priesthood was designed to be temporary in

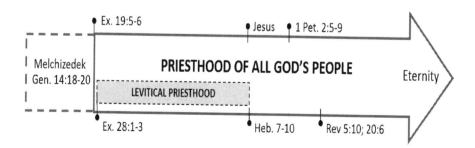

nature, the priestly order of Melchizedek appears to have been designed to be eternal (Hebrews 7:3, 21). In addition, Revelation 5:10 and 20:6 implies that our priestly role identity does not stop upon our death, but continues into the next life, into eternity. All of this is evidence to suggest that our priestly nature is core to our identity.

In a moment, I will provide a rationale for understanding our priestly mandate and explore some of the specific behaviors associated with our priesthood. Before I do that, let's take a slight digression to highlight the importance of the workplace as it relates to our priestly mandate.

Why the Workplace?

When I look at the weekly schedules of my friends, neighbors and colleagues, they spend 45-70 hours each week (of 168 possible) at

work, traveling to work, or preparing for work. Most of us spend more than half of our waking hours engaged in work-related activities. Most adults will spend more time at their workplace than they will with their family or

community; perhaps 85,000 hours, or more, over a lifetime.

When Jesus called us to follow him, he did not exclude the large percentage of our lives we spend at work. In fact, he probably had the workplace specifically in mind. Followers of Jesus must follow him in the workplace, as well as at home, and in the community. Our priestly nature informs us on how to follow Jesus in all three spheres, but let's concentrate on the workplace.

In the Scriptures, a priest was a member of the people he represented. A priest was an insider, not an outsider. As members of a workplace, followers of Jesus are uniquely positioned to represent Jesus there as insiders. Strangely, we often overlook and deprioritize the workplace as a place of ministry, which I will try to show, is the opposite of what God intended. For many of us, work is seen as a necessary evil, rather than an integral part of God's calling on our lives. Attitudes about the nature of work are mostly learned from our culture and therefore, are likely to differ from a biblical worldview of work.

I have lost count of the number of times people at church have told me they want to leave their secular jobs so they can serve God full-time. While I admire their longing to serve Jesus, this type of thinking is a consequence of wrongful thinking and theology. Full-time ministry is more a matter of our mindset than a matter of our actual job.

It is no secret that the majority of church staff and pastors spend 95% of their time serving, equipping, and coaching fellow Christians. This is good and beautiful, however they are typically not the ones spending much face to face time with non-Christians. Of course, all of us are called to serve fellow Christians at times, however, those in "secular" workplaces are typically much better positioned to minister to non-Christians than are pastors or people working for Christian organizations. I long for the day when followers of Jesus in secular workplaces such as public school systems, health sector, and construction sector are esteemed by the church as much as those in so-called full-time ministry. That will be a grand day. Unfortunately, too many churches unwittingly under esteem and underestimate the importance of the workplace in world missions when it is arguably the primary context for reaching the unreached.

As members of a workplace, we become community insiders of that workplace. It creates opportunity to build trust and open doors. Churches that are chock-full of workplace priests have the greatest opportunity to win their communities, cities, and nations for Jesus. We need to re-conceptualize our self-identity by learning what it means to be a priest, especially at the workplace. The local church needs to be a community for healing, esteeming, encouraging, and equipping workplace priests.

Questions for Reflection:

1. After reading Exodus 19:6 and 1 Peter 2:9, what do you think about the premise that all followers of Jesus are priests?

2. What does Hebrews 7:11-17 say about the priesthood?

3. Are you striving to live out your priestly identity? Why or why not?

4. What do you think would be the consequences if we honored workplace priests the same way we honor people who are in "full-time" ministry?

5. Can the term "workplace priest" be applied to people who are students, homemakers, self-employed, unemployed, or retired? Why or why not?

Chapter 3
Constructing an Identity Standard

An *identity standard* is the meanings and behavioral expectations we associate with a given role, such as priest, mother, boss, policeman, teacher, etc. Our initial identity standards are normally 100% derived from the family or cultures to which we belong. That is why in one culture being a policeman is thought of as a noble occupation but in another culture it can be perceived negatively. Identity standards are the behavioral expectations we associate with a role identity.

While the New Testament clearly outlines the identity standards for followers of Jesus, there are only a few passages that specifically address the identity standards associated with being a priest. However, since all followers of Jesus are priests, we can conclude that our priestly identity standard is simply a subset or dimension of being followers of Jesus.

So what aspects of following Jesus are particularly priestly? While there is no undisputable methodology to determine this, I took a three-pronged approach. My goal was to research the likely identity standards for our biblical priesthood in a way that is accurate, relevant, and applicable. Here is how I approached the subject.

Priestly Narratives in Scripture

First, I reviewed the narratives where the terms priest, priests, and priesthood appear in the Bible. I analyzed the text to identify  recurring activities and themes within the occupational category of priest. It included narratives from both non-Jewish and Jewish priests. In this process, I identified a primary occupational theme of "spiritual representation" and subcategories that included: worship, communication, ceremony, peacemaking, and service. I could align all of the priestly activities in the Old and New Testaments within one or more of these categories.

I compared these predominant priestly behaviors with New Testament identity standards for followers of Jesus. This resulted in a cluster of activities and attitudes that we can be reasonably confident compose key biblical identity standards that are particularly, but not exclusively, priestly. For example, Levitical priests represented both God on behalf of the people and the people on behalf of God. Prophets and many leaders of Israel did the same, so representation was not an exclusive domain reserved for priests. The Levites also led Israel in corporate worship, but worship leading was not solely the domain of priests. For example, even though King David was not a Levite, he also led Israel in worship. So worship and spiritual representation are particularly, but not exclusively, priestly in nature.

The Universal Callings of God

Second, I looked at what can be termed universal callings. The English word vocation comes from the Latin word meaning call. Today, Christians often use the terms "call" or "calling" to mean a specific appointment to a ministry or vocation. While Scripture occasionally uses it in that way, it more the exception rather than the rule. More commonly, the phrases "called to" or "chosen to" are literary devices used to emphasize different aspects of God's will for all his people. Thus, the term "universal callings" means purposes that God calls all his people to embrace or participate. They are not unique or limited to specific individuals, nor dependent on our gifts, context, or experience.

These "callings" are invitations to partner in God's purposes. They are aspects of how followers of Jesus can participate in his divine nature (1 Peter 4:13, 2 Peter 1:4). It is reasonable to assume these universal callings of God are linked to the identity standards for the universal priesthood of believers. Many universal callings exist in the Bible. I decided to limit myself to ten specific callings because the New Testament specifically links the terms "called to" or "chosen to" with most of them. I looked specifically at God's call to: salvation,[3] holiness,[4] love,[5] friendship,[6] peace,[7] service,[8] community,[9] work,[10] suffering,[11] and obedience.[12]

One could argue that these ten callings are actually commands, not just invitations. God's callings are indeed commands to obey, yet it is informative that they are frequently postured/presented as invitations, and thus I refer to them as such. To me, this hints at the gentle and generous nature of God. He wants us to respond on our own volition. Callings (like commands) need to be acted on. There are serious consequences if they are forgotten, ignored, or rejected.

2 Mandates:
Great Commission   New Commandment

---

[3] 1 Timothy 2:4, 2 Peter 3:9

[4] Ephesians 1:4, 5:27, 1 Peter 1:15-16

[5] Luke 10:27, Matthew 5:44

[6] John 15:13-15

[7] 1 Corinthians 7:15, Colossians 3:15, 2 Timothy 2:22

[8] Matthew 5:16, Ephesians 2:10, 1 Timothy 2:10, 5:10, 6:18

[9] Matthew 18:20, John 17:21, 1 Corinthians 12, Ephesians 4:4

[10] Genesis 1:27-28, 2:15,19-29, Colossians 3:17, 2 Thessalonians 3:10, 1 Timothy 5:8

[11] 1 Peter 2:21, 4:1 (specifically called to endure suffering as Jesus did)

[12] John 15:16

In regard to the priesthood, strong correlations exist between these universal callings of God and the priestly themes of representation, worship, peacemaking, and service. As I will explain later, it appears that God has made human agents (priests) the exclusive invitation bearers of his universal callings on planet earth. Therefore, the priest is privileged to invite his/her fellow human beings to RSVP to God's universal callings.

The Universal God-given Role Identities

Third, I studied seven identities that the Bible gives to all followers of Jesus. These included: child of God, disciple, saint, brother/sister, friend, servant, and ambassador. Like priest, these role identities are meant to be valid for all Christians. I found strong parallels between

these seven role identities and the priestly themes of representation, worship, peacemaking, and service. In fact, our priestly identity seems to summarize or encapsulate all seven of the other role identities in one. It is as if they are simply different dimensions or reflections of our priestly identity.

Ambassador vs. Priest

For example, consider the role identity of ambassador (or emissary). This role identity comes primarily from 2 Corinthians 5:20 where Paul says:

> We are therefore Christ's ambassadors, as though God were making his appeal through us. We implore you on Christ's behalf: Be reconciled to God.

The ambassadorship of all believers does not have the same universal acceptance among New Testament scholars as the priesthood of all believers. The role identity of ambassador is specifically mentioned only twice in the New Testament: once in 2 Corinthians 5:20 and once in Ephesians 6:20—both times by Paul. Scholars have different opinions about whether the plural pronoun "we" in 2 Corinthians 5:20 refers exclusively to Paul and Timothy, or is used in an inclusive sense (Paul and his readers).

In any case, it is interesting to consider the parallels between the identity standards of first-century ambassadors in the Hellenistic Roman Empire with the priestly themes of representation, peacemaking, and service. Both ambassadors and priests functioned as representatives of a sender. Both were responsible to communicate the sender's interests and were expected to behave in a manner that did not dishonor the sender. They also worked on teams to represent, communicate, and enhance relationships.

Further, both the priests and the ambassadors always belonged to the party (sender) they represented, as such they had similar vested interests as the sender. Compare the following first-century identity standards for ambassador and priest:

Ambassador or Emissary

An embassy consisted of an individual or an ad hoc group of representatives sent by an individual, organization, town, city state (the Sender) to travel to another individual, organization, town, or city state (the Receiver) either to mediate or promote the interests of the Sender. An ambassador was a member of such an embassy . . . Almost all the literary evidence about embassies implies that more than one representative was appointed, that is to say, embassies consisted of groups of men.

Bash (1997), pg 40.

Hebrew Priest

A male from the tribe of Levi, who worked with other priests under the supervision of the high priest, to carry out duties associated with worship at the temple in Jerusalem. The author of Hebrews writes, "Every high priest is selected from among men and is appointed to represent them in matters related to God, to offer gifts and sacrifice for sins. He is able to deal gently with those who are ignorant and are going astray, since he himself is subject to weakness. This is why he has to offer sacrifices for his own sins, as well as for the sins of the people." Hebrews 5:1-3

Bash (1997) presents a first-century identity standard for ambassadors that is strikingly similar with some of the identity standards of Hebrew priests of the same period. I suspect Paul purposefully contextualized his language and used the term "ambassador" rather than "priest" when writing to the Corinthians, who had a pagan background, because their identity standard for priest was shaped by the pagan society in Corinth, and not the Hebrew society in Israel. Whatever the case, the activities of representation, peacemaking, and service (as part of a team) were integral to what it meant to be both an emissary and a Hebrew priest. However, as mentioned earlier, the identity standard of New Covenant priests cannot be lifted directly from the Levitical priesthood. A new identity standard must be constructed.

It is reasonable to hypothesize that the identity standard for ambassador and the identity standard for priest represent different dimensions of a single identity standard - like two sides of the same coin. As ambassadors, we represent God (the Sender) to the people (the Receivers), while as priests we represent the people (the Senders) to God (the Receiver). Yet, in reality, the Hebrew priests of the Old Testament not only represented God on behalf of the Jewish people, they also represented the Jewish people on behalf of God. Likewise, in the Eastern Roman world, emissaries were just as likely to be sent by the people (of a town or city, for example) to the emperor (the Receiver), as they were to be sent from the emperor (the Sender) to the people (Bash, 1997).

A Working Identity Standard for Priest

From the three-pronged approach just described, I constructed the following working definition of a priest:

> A priest is someone who has God-given authority to represent God to people and represent people to God. Worship, obedience, and peacemaking are fundamental expectations God has of his priests.

Worship, holiness, peacemaking, representation, and service are five dominate themes of our priesthood. Within these themes I identified six behaviors of following Jesus that are definitely priestly in nature. I then constructed the acronym PRIEST (Praise, Reconcile, Invite, Encourage, Serve, Team up) to make these behaviors more explicit and easy to remember.[13] Woven like a thread that connects the six priestly behaviors is the idea that the priest is an *authorized insider*. Simultaneously a member of both the sender(s) and receiver(s). This dual association uniquely

---

[13] A shorter version of the P.R.I.E.S.T model was previously published in the July 2015 edition of *EMQ*, Wheaton, IL.

positions the priest to authoritatively represent God to people and represent people to God. [14]

I present these six behaviors as part of a biblically informed identity standard for what it fundamentally means to be a priest. I encourage the reader to engage with the following chapters as one might consume a salmon fillet - alert for the inevitable bones. These are not new ideas but rather a new framework for reemphasizing an old idea.

---

[14] I decided not to include a discussion on the role of priests in administering Christian rites or sacraments such as communion, baptism, etc.). There are a wide range of informed opinions and traditions on this topic, none of which that I know of are particularly incompatible with my thesis. Suffice to say, participating in the Lord's Supper is one way we proclaim our Lord's death (1 Corinthians 11:26) and according to 1 Pet.2:9, proclaiming is one of the fundamental duties of our priesthod. Participating in the Lord's Supper is an important habit for followers of Jesus.

Questions for Reflection:

1. Why did the author use a three pronged approach in constructing an identity standard for priest instead of just studying the Levitical priesthood?

2. What are the universal callings mentioned in the following verses? 1 Timothy 2:4, Ephesians 1:4, 5:27, Luke 10:27, John 15:13-15, 1 Corinthians 7:15, Colossians 3:15, Matthew 5:16, Ephesians 2:10, Matthew 18:20, John 17:21, Colossians 3:17, and John 15:16?

3. The author considers these universal callings to be universal invitations. What are your thoughts?

4. Which, if any, of our God-given role identities do you find most difficult to embrace or internalize? Why?

5. What are the risks of constructing an identity standard for the role of priest from scattered Bible narratives and research? What are the risks of not doing it?

Chapter 4
Praise and Pray

Priests are people of praise and prayer. They are foremost worshipers of God. Praise is perhaps the most explicit behavior connected to our priestly identity in the New Testament because it is specifically linked to 1 Peter 2:9 (emphasis added):

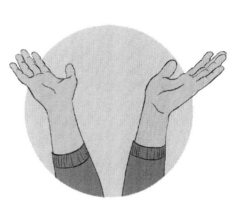

> But you are a chosen people, a royal priesthood, a holy nation, a people belonging to God, that you may *declare the praises of him* who called you out of darkness into his wonderful light.

The Greek word *exaggello,* translated here as "declare," also means to "proclaim or show forth" and implies proactive and loud verbalization. The Greek word *aretê*, translated as "praises" also means moral goodness, valor, virtue, or excellence.[15] Priests are to declare, proclaim, and show forth God's praises (e.g. his moral

---

[15] According to Strong's Hebrew and Greek Dictionaries

goodness, valor, virtues, and excellence). The people of God are to be people of praise, worship, and prayer. Declaring or proclaiming God's praise is fundamental to what it means to be priestly.[16] It is who we are and what we do. Priests are to be people of worship in both actions and attitudes.[17] Praise and worship are integral to the job description of being priests.

Does this means we are to walk around our workplace loudly singing praise to God? Maybe, but I suspect this isn't an option in many workplaces. More likely, at the workplace, it points to inner attitudes of praise. At work, praise likely manifests itself as we maintain attitudes of thankfulness, gratitude, service, humility, optimism, and expectation. Let's look at this further.

Work as Worship

Romans 12:1 suggests that worship is living in a mindset of surrender to God's will. Such a mindset will allow work itself to be an act of worship. As workplace priests, we understand that ultimately our accountability is to God and thus we always strive to act in ways that please and glorify God at all times…no matter

---

[16] Proclaiming God's praises is a more compelling interpretation of 1 Peter 2:9b than proclaiming the gospel
[17] Also see Acts 2:11, 1 Corinthians 11:26

what we do and no matter if anyone is watching or not. As Paul reminds us in Colossians 3:23:

> Whatever you do, work at it with all your heart, as working for the Lord, not for men, since you know you will receive an inheritance from the Lord as a reward. It is the Lord Christ you are serving.

It does not matter if we clean toilets or lead a Fortune 500 company—either way, work can be, but is not automatically, worship. It depends on our attitude. For work to be worship we need to realign our attitude towards work so that it is consistent with God's vision of work.

God assigned work to Adam before the fall (Genesis 1:28, 2:15) and thus work was always part of God's plan for mankind. While sin affects work, it does not transform the fundamental nature of work from a blessing to a curse. We should understand that work was designed by God as a means of partnering with him. Much has been written about the *theology of work* and *work as worship* so I will not repeat it all here. I encourage the reader to dig deeply into the theology of work as it is fundamental to our priestly nature.[18]

The parable of the three stonemasons speaks to the concept of work as worship. Three men were working in a stone quarry. Each appeared to be doing identical tasks. When asked what they were doing, they gave three distinct answers.

> "I am cutting stone," the first one replied.
> "I am building a cathedral," the second one said.
> "I am worshiping God," the third one answered.

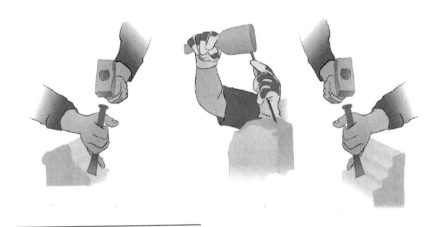

---

[18] For example see: http://www.reframecourse.com or http://www.workasworshipnetwork.org/ or https://www.theologyofwork.org or http://www.intheworkplace.com/ or https://tifwe.org/ or google "theology of work" or "work as worship" to explore the many books, articles, sermon notes, blogs, and videos that discuss this key concept.

While all the responses are true, which response do you suppose best represents the perspective of a workplace priest? It is hard to imagine being an effective workplace priest unless we can embrace the attitude that our work itself is an expression of worship. This can be especially difficult if we do not enjoy our work and/or the people we work with. Does this describes you? If so, you may need to change either your job or your attitude. In any case, most of us need major changes in our attitudes towards work.

Praise is one aspect of worship and work is another. Prayer is a third. Prayer is one of the key ways we communicate with God. According to 1 Thessalonians 5:16-18 we should be praying continuously, which implies that we can pray even when we are doing other things, even while we work.

The workplace priest is an intercessor because it is part of our representative function. Since we represent our workplace before God we have the role of continuously interceding to God on behalf of our colleagues, customers, suppliers, etc. We have the responsibility and privilege to communicate to God with praise, intercession, and thanksgiving for the people and needs that arise in our workplace. It is the workplace priest's job to represent his or her colleagues before God in prayer as an insider and member of the workplace.

I suggest that as priests we have the same basic responsibilities, whether we are working alongside Christians or non-Christians. The priest prays, "Jesus, how do I represent you here?" and not just "Jesus, how can I share the gospel here?" Learning to "listen" in prayer is a skill we must develop so we can more effectively represent Jesus before both Christians and non-Christians. Learning the Scriptures and meditating on how to apply what we learn in our daily lives is critical if we are to embrace our priestly nature at work.

Questions for Reflection:

1. Is praiselessness a symptom of spiritual unhealthiness? Why or why not?
2. What might you do to become a more worshipful person? What adjustments, if any, to your attitude and actions need to happen?
3. What is your reaction to the idea that work should be understood as an act of worship? What Scripture would you use to support or refute this idea?
4. How would you describe your local culture's attitude of work? In what ways, if any, does it align with Scripture? In what ways, if any, does it not?
5. What are some practical ways you can become a strong intercessor for your workplace?

Chapter 5

Reconcile

Priests are peacemakers. To reconcile is to make peace. Peacemaking is high on God's agenda. We worship the God of peace (Hebrews 13:20) and the people of God are his primary agents of peace (2 Cor 5:18-20). We are priests in the order of Melchizedek "king of Salem" or "king of peace" (Hebrews 7:2). It is therefore the business of priests  to be peacemakers. At the workplace, peacemaking has three primary dimensions.

Three Levels of Reconciliation at Work

First, it is incumbent upon priests to be reconciled with God themselves. We must not only trust Jesus for our personal salvation, but we must also be pursuing obedience and personal holiness. This does not mean priests are perfect. Rather, it means we should be quick to repent, and in pursuit of being a friend of God. Envy, pride, laziness, gossip, slander, bitterness, and malicious talk are incompatible with our priestly identity. They are unholy and unbecoming to followers of Jesus. Rather, we purpose to live holy, exemplary lives surrendered to Jesus at home, in the community and at work.

Second, and related to the first, it is essential for priests to take the "planks" out of their own eyes before helping others take the "specks" out of their eyes (Matthew 7:3-5). In other words, we must be committed to personal holiness and to pursuing peace in our own broken relationships.

Our relationships with our fellow humans is in many ways a reflection of our relationship with God. For example, the Scripture teaches that it is not possible to love God yet hate our brothers (1 John 4:20). Like oil and water, hating fellow humans is incompatible with loving God. Therefore, we need to do *everything in our power* to pursue peace with all people (Hebrews 12:14). Forgiving those who have wronged us is a sign that we are his followers (Matthew 6:14, 18:35). Unwillingness to forgive is a sign that we may not be a follower of Jesus. Forgiveness is one step toward reconciliation, but true reconciliation always requires all parties in the conflict to participate. When one party in a conflict is unwilling to engage, then true reconciliation is unattainable. Do not let that person be you if you claim to follow Jesus. Pursuing peace is a scared obligation of all God's people and thus central to our priestly nature.

An Early Workplace Experience

As a young man, I once had a boss for whom it was difficult to work under. He bullied those who reported to him and frequently ridiculed and belittled us. He took credit for other peoples' work and stepped on his staff to climb the corporate ladder. At that time I knew enough about biblical peacemaking to forgive him, and I did, many times, yet somehow I was still filled with resentment. Every time I tried to pray or have personal devotions, my anger would well-up and make it very difficult to pray or read the Bible.

In obedience to what I read in Scripture in Matthew 5:38-48, 7:1-6, I determined to reflect more deeply on my own attitudes and actions. I realized that I needed to own my shortcomings (even though in my eyes they seemed minor compared to my boss) and repent from them. I realized that I had become slack in some of my work because I was so demotivated. I realized that down deep, I had been working to please my boss and not Jesus. I had my own set of ambitions that appeared to be threatened or thwarted by my boss. I resolved to reset my affections on Jesus even if it meant setting aside my personal ambitions for more responsibility and influence at work. I resolved to do what was right based on my understanding of God's will and secondly, what seemed best for the company. One specific action was that I resolved not to participate in the office gossip, nor to slander my boss. Instead, I determined to inject positive comments about him whenever I could. He did, after all, have many positive traits, even if they seemed shadowed by his dark side. I also proactively prayed for God to bless him. These actions were counter intuitive to how if felt emotionally, but they were the practical ways I could apply Jesus' teaching in Matthew 5:44, where Jesus tells us to love our enemies, and to pray for those who persecute us.

↳ Does love include peace?

Within a few days, my anger toward my boss had dissolved. My mind was no longer dominated by resentment. I had a new sense of mission at work. I wanted Jesus to be pleased with me even more than I wanted to please my boss or satisfy my own ambitions. Two weeks later, my boss invited me into his office. I assumed I was going to get chewed out for something. *At least he is going to do it privately this time,* I thought to myself. He had me sit down, and shut the door. "Scott you are a Christian, aren't you?" he asked. "Yeeess, siirr." I answered as I braced myself, expecting to be ridiculed. "I thought so," he replied. "I wanted to let you know that I committed my life to Jesus this weekend during a church retreat!" I could hardly believe my ears. I was a little reluctant to believe him. However, in the days and weeks that followed, everyone in the office witnessed changes. It was amazing. I had changed, too. I had learned an important lesson in removing the plank from my own eyes and the transformational power of forgiveness, even though I had no real hope of truly reconciling with my boss. I am not sure who changed more, me or my boss. I received more than I had hoped for, including a long overdue promotion.

Pursuing peace within our own circle of relationships helps qualify us for the third dimension of peacemaking at the workplace, namely facilitating peace and reconciliation between work colleagues or clients.

Interpersonal conflicts at the workplace are one of the primary sources of stress, job dissatisfied, inefficiency, and leaving jobs prematurely. Unresolved conflicts are also extremely detrimental to the emotional health of staff and to business operations. Mediating conflict resolution at work is a learned skill which everyone should be trained in and some of you will excel at. There are some great books[19] on practical peacemaking and workplace conflict resolution. I encourage the reader to equip themselves to be peacemakers at work.

Those are the three dimensions of reconciliation at work. The first two of which are foundational to everything else written in this

---

[19] I can recommend Rick Love's *Peace Catalysts* (InterVarsity Press, 2014), Ken Sande's *The Peacemaker* (Baker Book House, 1992) and Daniel Dana's *Conflict Resolution* (McGraw-Hill) for learning about practical peacemaking.

book. "But wait," you may ask, "didn't you forget the most important kind of peacemaking?"

> What about the role of helping reconcile people to God? Shouldn't priests also be preaching the gospel of peace to colleagues and clients in the workplace?

I will address this in the next section.

Questions for Reflection:

Rom 12:18

1. How do you respond to the premise that pursuing peace is fundamental to our priestly nature?
2. Do you currently make pursuing peace a high priority? Can you share an example?
3. What does it mean to "take the plank from our own eye"? Can you share a personal example?
4. Take a minute to consider if there is someone you need to forgive or reconcile with?
5. Choose one or more of the following verses (Matthew 5:9, Matthew 5:23-24, Matthew 5:25-26, Matthew 5: 38-42, Matthew 6:14-15, Matthew 18:15-17, Romans 14:19, Galatians 6:1, Hebrews 12:14, Psalm 34:14). What insight does it give about peacemaking?

Chapter 6

Invite

Priests are invitation bearers. This is a reflection of our function as representatives of God to the people in our workplace. We are message bearers entrusted[20] with the Good News that God wants peace and friendship with all the people in our community, family, and

workplace. In fact, God wants peace with everyone on planet earth, but let's start with the people we have access to first. Of course, before a person can have peace with God, they need to hear and accept God's terms for peace. This is called the *ministry of reconciliation.*[21] We invite people to have peace with God on God's terms. This is one of our key responsibilities as a priests.

One cannot understand peace unless he knew they are in war/conflict

Invitations and the Ministry of Reconciliation

I find it helpful to think of the ministry of reconciliation as consisting of three distinct and somewhat sequential phases. The

---

[20] 2 Corinthians 5:18
[21] 2 Corinthians 5:19-20

first phase is an invitation to *come hear* the Word of God. The second phase involves hearing, discussing, and explaining the Word of God. The third phase is an invitation to *respond* to the Word of God. In this paradigm, the Good News is sandwiched between two distinct invitations: the invitation to *come hear* and the invitation to *respond*. We normally proclaim the Word of God only to those who are willing to hear it. Therefore, the first step is to invite people to a place where they can listen and learn what God has to say. It does not need to be hard or stressful to invite people to hear the Word of God. However, it normally requires us to:

- Ask good questions (to people and God)
- Listen carefully (to people and God)
- Be ready to invite the person(s) to a setting that is appropriate and accessible for them to hear

In this chapter I want to focus our discussion on the role of invitations. Particularly how to invite people to "come hear" the Word of God by first inviting them to hear smaller "bite size" parts of Scripture. Faith comes as people *hear* (Romans 10:17). God's Word. Experiencing miracles, having supernatural dreams[22] or

---

[22] See Breslin and Jones (2004), *Understanding Dreams from God*

being beneficiaries of good deeds or other acts of love can be very important in helping people in their journey towards Jesus but they are not enough on their own. At some point in time they also need to *hear* the Word of God since faith comes *from hearing* (Matthew 10:9-17).

Let's discuss how invitations, appropriate to the context and to the person, are critical elements to the ministry of reconciliation. In my experience, invitations that prepare a person to "come hear" takes just as much work, boldness, patience, and discernment as sharing the Word of God.

First, let's consider how invitations were integral to the public ministry of Billy Graham, perhaps the most famous preacher of the 20th Century. When large crowds came to hear Billy Graham, typically the largest percentage of the audience were already Christians. The second largest percentage where non-Christian friends and relatives of the first group who had been invited to "come hear" Billy Graham. The smallest percentage of the audience were non-Christians who showed up to the meetings alone by themselves. But even those people had received invitations to "come hear" via a friend or perhaps an advertisement in the public media. The point being, everyone attending a Billy Graham meeting came because they were willing to "come hear." Practically no one showed up at a Billy Graham meeting by accident. The invitation process involved months of prayer and

Conduct so oikos

preparation by the Billy Graham team and local churches who hosted the meetings. Appropriate advertisements to "come hear" were always integral to the success of Billy Graham meetings. This principle is demonstrated in Scriptures and equally valid when the ministry of reconciliation is done on a smaller scale or one-to-one basis. As such, workplace priests must learn how to appropriately extend various types of invitations to their work colleagues and clients. Let's look more closely at this idea of being *inviters*.

Readiness to Hear

In Matthew 22:1-14, Jesus likens the kingdom of heaven to a wedding feast where the king sends out his servants to invite everyone to the wedding banquet. People need to know that they are wanted and welcome to God's Kingdom. The choice to come or not is up to them. Our job is to let them know they are invited... perhaps at times even pleading for them to come, but it is their choice to come or not. Appropriate invitations probe people's readiness to hear the Gospel. Interestingly, in Matthew 7:6, the Scriptures warn us to avoid sharing sacred truth with those who are not ready or receptive. This is one reason why appropriate invitations are so important. We can test and see if people might be receptive to the Gospel by extending invitations that seem to fit the situation and the audience.

A good friend of mine likes this process to feeding ducks at the park. Common sense restrains most of us from throwing a whole loaf of bread to the ducks. Instead, we rip off appropriate bite-size pieces of bread and throw them out to the ducks. If the ducks are interested, they will gobble them up and step closer with each bite. It is similar when we extend invitations that have a spiritual or sacred dimension. We start with appropriate bite-size bits of the kingdom, not the whole loaf. As people show more interest and appetite for the sacred, we share more. Since people are more complex and amazing than ducks we need to have an array of different invitations that are appropriate to different people and contexts.

One way to God-Jesus, Many ways to Jesus

For example, we can invite people to pray with us, read a book, share a meal, watch a movie, meet our Christian friends, come to church, or join a Bible study. The possibilities are endless. We invite people to these various events based on a number of factors, including what is available and what we determine is appropriate to their situation. We try to invite people to take steps toward Jesus appropriate to their openness and appetite. It takes boldness, discernment, and intentionality on our part but it is not particularly hard nor require the gift of evangelism.

Take for example, a Christian nightclub musician who wants to be more proactive in his priestly identity at work. He might take a short pause before a song and say, "I wrote this while I was struggling with my faith. If anyone wants to hear the whole story, I'll be at the bar after the performance." Out of 45 people in the audience, four meet with him at the bar to hear his story (or maybe they are just hoping for a free drink). Three of the four already know each other. He tells his story (i.e. testimony) and asks questions to get to know the four strangers. During the conversation, he learns that one of the four has lost his job and asks if he can pray for him. Toward the end of the evening, the musician decides to invite all four to a weekly Bible study. Two say yes, and they exchange contact information.

Here's another example. A male nurse notices that one of his work colleagues is stressed over the relationship with her partner. After praying about the situation, he decides to invite his colleague to read *The Five Love Languages* by Gary Chapman. He mentions how much the book helped him in his relationship with his wife. The colleague accepts the book gratefully.

One week later, the nurse invites his colleague (and her partner) over for dinner to discuss the highlights of the book as couples.

The colleague and her partner come for dinner and discuss the book. Toward the end of the evening, her partner makes a comment about the last chapter, where the author briefly mentions how his own marriage struggles helped him rediscover his need for God. This leads to an interesting conversation, and the nurse decides to ask his colleague and her partner if they would be interested in studying the New Testament together to discuss the topic further. They both say yes.

Notice that at each level of invitation, the number of people may go down but the content level of what is shared goes up.[23] This is to be expected. In the musician's case, the first invitation allowed people to determine whether they wanted to hear more or not. Similarly, the nurse invited his colleague to read a book because he noticed she was struggling with a relationship.

Personally, I think one of the most important things we can do is invite people to read and discuss the Bible together. I prefer to start by looking at the life and teachings of Jesus in Matthew, Mark, Luke, or John. Otherwise, I might focus on a topic that is of

---

[23] Breslin, S. (2007), *Church Planting Tracking and Analysis Tool*, (EMQ, Wheaton, IL, October 2007), pp. 508-515

particular interest to them. The Discovery Bible Study (DBS)[24] approach is an effective and easy-to-learn method for leading Bible discussions with individuals and small groups. But I would always do this outside the workplace and certainly not during work hours.

Salty Statements

At any workplace, there are almost always people to whom we can extend some sort of invitation that is appropriate to the context. It requires us to be both reactive and proactive. In Colossians 4:5-6, Paul emphasized the importance of being ready to respond to opportunities:

> Be wise in the way you act toward outsiders; make the most of every opportunity. Let your conversation be always full of grace, seasoned with salt, so that you may know how to answer everyone.

Here, Paul instructs us to be wise and proactive and for our words to be gracious and 'salty'. His advice is directed to how we should act towards both *outsiders* (i.e. those not yet following Jesus) and *everyone*. Since work colleagues and customers come under at

---

[24] A Google search will lead to many articles which explain how to lead a Discovery Bible Study.

least one of these two categories this is good advice about how we should act at work. We may or may not know all the people in our workplace, but being part of the same workplace gives us a context to meet and interact with *outsiders* and *everyone*. I proactively "season my conversation with salt" by making statements that have a spiritual dimension and/or by asking questions that probe to learn if a person is interested in talking about the things of God. For example, I might say something like:

- There is an interesting passage in the Bible that has influenced the way I think about immigration/child raising/marriage/money/etc. [This assumes I am part of a conversation about immigration/child raising/marriage/money/etc.]
- Your situation reminds me of an ancient proverb I memorized. [This statement assumes I have memorized or can paraphrase a relevant proverb.]
- I really had a good laugh on Sunday over the story/joke our pastor used to introduce his sermon.
- Can I pray for you about that situation?

I try not to force "salty" statements into contexts they do not fit, but we learn by doing. You will not always get it right. In any case, what I say is informed by the context of the conversation, not by my agenda to put out a certain message. After I make a statement or question I don't automatically provide the answer. I normally wait for the person to whom I am talking to invite me to go on. If they do invite me to continue, I may ask, "Are you sure?" Depending on the context, timing, and openness, I might later extend an additional invitation, such as:

- If you want, I would be happy to talk about that more in depth after work.
- Would you be interested in joining a group of my friends who meet once a week to investigate what the Bible says?
- I'd like to introduce you to a person that I think can answer your questions much better than I. What do you think?
- Would you like to join me Saturday morning for a special breakfast meeting at church where the speaker will be talking about xx?

I suggest that inviting people to "come hear" is normally more appropriate to the workplace than extensive sharing of the Gospel. The workplace is often a space for sharing bite-size bits of bread, but normally not a place for sharing the whole loaf. This has largely to do with time constraints, employer expectations, appropriateness, and context. As far as I can tell, Jesus, Peter, and Paul only preached in the temple, synagogues, river bank, or other spaces where people gathered, on their own volition, to hear.[25] The workplace is normally not such a place. The workplace is normally better suited for 'salty' conversations and for appropriate invitations to "come hear" in another space. Therefore, let's be committed to growing our competence as inviters at our workplace.

---

[25] Jonah on the other hand, appears to have preached to the people of Nineveh without using invitations or questions to probe their readiness to hear. It just goes to show that God has many ways to accomplish his will. However, I am not convinced that Jonah should be our primary role model for the ministry of reconciliation.

Questions for Reflection:

1. What are your thoughts about being an inviter? Does it make sense to you?

2. Do you agree with the author's interpretation of Matthew 7:6, in that we should use appropriate invitations and questions to probe people's readiness before sharing the Gospel? Why or why not?

3. Can you think of any examples in the Bible in which followers of Jesus used invitations or questions to probe people's readiness?

4. How can we develop our invitation skills?

5. Do you agree with the author's suggestion that the workplace can be a great place for appropriate invitations to "come hear" but not normally an appropriate place for preaching? Why or why not?

Chapter 7

Encourage

Priests bless and encourage people. *Blessing* is the second priestly behavior explicitly connected with our priestly identity. Melchizedek, the priest of God Most High, blessed Abram with both deeds and words.[26] He proactively went out to bless Abram by bringing bread and wine  and invoking a verbal blessing. The verbal blessing went like this:

> Blessed be Abram by God Most High, Creator of heaven and earth. And blessed be God Most High, who delivered your enemies into your hand.

Words of Blessing

God wants his priests to be proactive and habitual in blessing others. To do so is fundamentally consistent with our priestly nature. Numbers 6:22-27 has become known as the *priestly*

---

[26] Genesis 14:18-20

blessing because Aaron and his sons were commanded to use these words when blessing the people of Israel. The Lord said to Moses,

> Tell Aaron and his sons, 'This is how you are to bless the Israelites. Say to them: *The LORD bless you and keep you; the Lord make his face shine on you and be gracious to you; the LORD turn his face toward you and give you peace.*'

This blessing is prescribed in a way that reminds me of the Lord's Prayer in Matthew 6:9-13, where Jesus says, "This, then, is how you should pray," and then he provides the phraseology for the prayer. Historically, the priestly blessing and the Lord's Prayer have both been memorized verbatim as well as used a general outline for blessing and prayer. Notice that the priestly blessings of both Melchizedek and Aaron invoke or summon the benevolence or goodness of God on the subject(s) being blessed.

Blessing people is a different ministry than praying for people. A blessing is a verbal pronouncement that somehow transfers or enhances the receiver with the goodness of God. Our heavenly Father has given the authority and responsibility to his people, his priests to bless others. It is part of our agency on behalf of God's Kingdom. It is an awesome responsibility to be tasked to recognize and affirm the affection and image of God in others.

Unfortunately, it has become a lost art in most of our societies. It is rarely practiced or promoted even in church least of all the workplace. Today, we are more accustomed to hear cursing, belittling, and slander at work. Let's change that by being a people who are committed to verbally bless and encourage others routinely at home and at work. After all, it is what all God's priests are supposed to do.

Words of Encouragement and Affirmation

Offering words of encouragement and affirmation are other priestly actions within the same genre as blessing. [27] In part, this means we affirm qualities we know to be godly that we see in others. As 'image bearers' of God (Genesis 1:26-27), when we notice the image of God shining through a fellow human, we can verbally affirm it to them.

This is priestly work; both to notice it and to affirm it, whether the objects of the affirmation are Christians or non-Christians. It is important to remember that God blesses even bad people. [28] Since God is kind even to the ungrateful and the wicked[29] we should be

---

[27] Ephesians 4:29, Colossians 3:16; 4:5, Luke 4:22
[28] Psalms 145:9, Matthew 5:45, Acts 14:17
[29] Luke 6:35-36, 1 Peter 3:9

too. In fact, we are called to love even our enemy (Matthew 5:43-48). Also, the theological doctrine of *common grace* addresses this issue. Many aspects of God's grace benefit all humankind, no matter what their faith or practice. I appreciate the way theologian and peace activist, Dr. Rick Love describes it:[30]

> By common grace, unbelievers do good; in fact they often do amazing things. And we should see God's hand in it. We should be grateful that God's common grace operates in every friendship, every act of kindness, every scientific discovery, and every technological advance. For all of this is ultimately from God . . . God *is* working in people around us. His beauty shines through them— even though imperfectly and without them realizing that God is the one who is actually working through them.

I believe our priestly identity makes it natural for us to recognize and celebrate godly behavior even when we witness it in people who are not followers of Jesus. Any time we witness godliness is a time to affirm and celebrate. As workplace priests, we can affirm the words, actions, and attitudes that we know please God when we see them in others, no matter what their faith (if any). We can

---

[30] http://peace-catalyst.net/blog/post/common-grace--common-ground--and-the-common-good--part-1

simply say, "I admire your generous heart," or "You handled that difficult customer with dignity" or "Well done on that job." This is not empty flattery, but spiritual affirmation and encouragement. It is godliness in action. It is priestly.

I focus my encouragement not on people's outward appearance (although that can be good sometimes too) but on character, attitudes, and behavior. Since all people are created in the image of God, I try to speak words of affirmation when I recognize God's image in them. I often pray "Lord give me a word of blessing or affirmation for X (name) right now." As I get to know my work colleagues, I learn to shape my words of encouragement to fit their circumstances.

That being said, there also will be times when we must speak up against workplace injustice, abuse, and dishonesty. It might mean blowing the whistle on acts of injustice or corruption or taking a stand against gossip and slander. Jesus could be pretty tough, but he always acted in love on behalf of others. I touch on this topic a bit more in the next section.

Questions for Reflection:

1. What do blessings and words of affirmation have in common? How are they different?

2. Is encouraging others something you can do easily at most workplaces? Why or why not?

3. How is blessing and encouraging people (including non-Christians) consistent with the doctrine of common grace? See Matthew 5:43-48.

4. Write out a blessing in your own words. How else can you train yourself to be an encourager?

5. What do you think about the author's contention that blessing and encouraging others (including non-Christians) is part of our priestly mandate or duty?

Chapter 8
Serve

Priests serve God and people. Throughout the New Testament, followers of Jesus are called servants. Serving requires surrender. It means surrendering our own plans, ambitions, and thinking to  God. It means submitting to his leadership in our life and following where he leads. In other words, we are called to die to self in order to live for God. In Romans 12:1-2 it says it like this:

> Therefore, I urge you brothers, in view of God's mercy, to offer your bodies as living sacrifices, holy and pleasing to God – this is your spiritual act of worship. Do not conform any longer to the pattern of this world, but be transformed by the renewing of your mind. Then you will be able to test and approve what God's will is – his good, pleasing and perfect will.

Serving is fundamental to following Jesus and therefore fundamental to our priesthood. Even Jesus, our Great High Priest, embraced the identity and duties of a servant.[31] Consider Philippians 2:3-6:

> Do nothing out of selfish ambition or vain conceit, but in humility consider others better than yourselves. Each of you should look not only to your own interests, but also to the interests of others. Your attitude should be the same as that of Christ Jesus: Who, being in very nature God, did not consider equality with God something to be grasped, but made himself nothing, taking the very nature of a servant.

Jesus taught that a servant is not greater than his master, nor is a messenger greater than the one who sent him.[32] Followers of Jesus are to be servants because Jesus was a servant. Like all God-given identities, both vertical and horizontal dimensions exist within our servant identity.

Vertical and Horizontal Obligations

The vertical dimension highlights that we are servants of God. We are to submit to God's agenda and strive to know and obey his

---

[31] Matthew 12:18, Philippians 2:6-8
[32] John 13:16

will.[33] Even in the Old Testament, obeying God was a prerequisite to priestly identity of his people.[34]

The horizontal dimension highlights that we are also servants of people. In this regard, the Scriptures command us to treat other people as more important than ourselves. The servant theme appears repeatedly when we study the priestly narratives of Scripture. It is a role that is others oriented. Selfishness, greed, and arrogance are contradictory to our servant identity and therefore unpriestly. Workplace priests serve God and humans.

Suffering for Doing Right

It might be appropriate to include a comment here about the calling of followers of Jesus to bear up under unjust suffering in work and in life. This is one of the universal callings for followers of Jesus. This is specifically mentioned in 1 Peter 2:18-24. Then in 1 Peter 4:1, we are told it is not only commendable to suffer for doing good, but it is something we can plan on. It is part of our calling as followers of Jesus. The context here is not necessarily suffering persecution for being Christians, but any suffering for doing what

---

[33] Romans 12:1-3
[34] Exodus 19:5-6

is right or good. Both non-Christians and Christians can suffer for doing what is right or good.

It is naïve to expect that doing what is right will always be rewarded here on earth. When we suffer unjustly, it does not mean God has rejected us or is punishing us. As mentioned earlier, we are forewarned in Scripture that we should expect to suffer for doing what is good. We are *called* to bear up and endure such suffering because Jesus did. If we are fortunate enough to be occasionally rewarded here on earth for doing what is right or good, we should consider it a pleasant exception, rather than a right.

This can have significant implications for the workplace priest. We may find ourselves in situations in which we are asked to do things we believe are morally wrong. We may be faced with corrupt officials or suppliers who demand bribes. We may have a boss who asks us to do things we do not believe are right. We may experience strong peer pressure to slow down or stop work when the boss is not looking. We might feel morally obligated to "blow the whistle" on workplace misbehavior. The ways we might take a stand, and ultimately suffer for it are many. Suffering is sometimes part of the cost of maintaining a clear conscience (Acts 24:16). That being said, we should make two qualifications.

First, our conscience is an important but imperfect moral benchmark. We cannot rely on it as our sole barometer for what is right and wrong. Scripture, rightfully understood, and godly wisdom also need to be applied. The Scriptures give precedence to "love" as one of our most important moral barometers and, therefore, we need to take action based on what is most loving. Second, in my own experience, I have frequently been successful in negotiating alternative solutions with bosses and officials who have initially asked me to do things that would have violated my conscience. We can often find win-win alternatives when we look for them. Disobeying earthly authorities (work or government) is not something that should be done flippantly, but only after all other alternatives have been exhausted. Then we must face the consequences with courage and humility.

A Student of the Word of God

Being a servant implies that our agenda is to advance the agenda of our master. Similarly, being a priest is about representing and serving the agenda of God. How can we know the agenda of God without being familiar with the priorities and purposes of God? Therefore, it is incumbent on the servant-priest to be a lifelong student of the Bible and an active participant in the community of Jesus followers. Being a disciple (i.e. student) is as integral to our priestly nature as being a servant. Interestingly, in John 15:15 Jesus says he will call us his friends rather than servants:

> I no longer call you servants, because a servant does not know his master's business. Instead, I have called you friends, for everything that I learned from my Father I have made known to you.

Being a disciple, a servant, and a friend of God are different dimensions of our priestly nature.

Questions for Reflection:

1. What are some practical ways being a servant of God will affect your behavior at work?

2. What are some practical ways being a servant of people will affect your behavior at work?

3. On a scale of 1-10, with 1 being self-oriented and 10 being others-oriented, where do you put yourself? Why? On that same scale, where do you think others would put you? Why?

4. In what ways are you a servant at work?

5. In light of John 15:15, what is the "business" of our master Jesus?

Chapter 9
Team Up

Workplace priests team up.
They are an integral part of a
community with other followers
of Jesus. Teaming up is
explicitly connected to our
identity as priests. Three times
the plurality of the priesthood is
emphasized in 1 Peter 2:9:

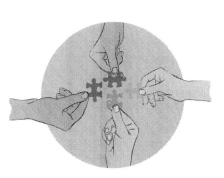

> You are a chosen *people*, a royal priesthood, a holy
> *nation*, a *people* belonging to God . . ." The priesthood
> to which we belong was designed to function as a
> community.

The "One Another" Commands

The New Testament gives us the "one another" commands that
highlight our mutual obligation to be in community.[35] For
example:

---

[35] Romans 12:4-6 also speaks of teamwork.

- Love one another (John 13:34-35, 5:12,17)
- Be devoted to one another (Romans 12:10)
- Be at peace with one another (Mark 9:50, 1 Thes 5:13)
- Be kind to one another (1 Thes 5:15)
- Live in harmony with one another (Romans 12:16)
- Accept one another (Romans 15:7)
- Instruct one another (Romans 15:14)
- Bear with one another (Ephesians 4:2, Colossians 3:13)
- Speak with psalms, hymns and spiritual songs to one another (Ephesians 5:19)
- Forgive one another (Colossians 3:13)
- Confess your sins to one another (James 5:16)
- Encourage one another (Hebrews 3:13)
- Pray for one another (James 5:16)
- Offer hospitality to one another (1 Peter 4:9)
- Serve one another (1 Peter 4:10)

These commands, and others like them, presuppose that followers of Jesus are teamed up with one another. As a plurality of priests, we are better at representing, communicating, peacemaking, worshipping, obeying, and serving than we are on our own. As such, being a priest implies working as part of a team. Even our prayers somehow have greater impact when we join together with others (Matthew 18:19-20). God designed the priesthood to be a community of people working together. It is a team sport. It does not work the way it was designed unless we team up with others. As we learn to work as a team, conflicts will likely emerge. This is an opportunity to develop your commitment and skills in peacemaking.

Ideally, the local church is an expression of priests who team up to fulfill our priestly role in the local community. Church meetings can equip and encourage the congregation of priests to fulfill their priestly responsibilities at home, work, and in the community.

Organizing Ourselves at the Workplace

In addition, priests benefit from teaming up with other priests in their workplace, and with others in their vocation. Priests who belong to the same workplace or same vocation group are especially able to encourage and equip each other. Teachers and school administrators should seek out other like-minded colleagues at school. Doctors, nurses, and other staff can form "communities of practice"[36] at their hospital or clinic. Priests who work as sales people at shopping centers, and employees in

---

[36] Groups of people who share a concern or a passion for something they do, and learn how to do it better as they interact regularly

factories can organize themselves so as to better fulfill their sacred duties as workplace priests. Different churches within a city can help facilitate the organization of priestly communities of practice by providing meeting space for weekly meetings or at other times.

One Example

In my own case, as a young management consultant working for a large international auditing partnership in Washington, D.C., I organized a handful of Christians to have a weekly lunch together. We prayed for and encouraged each other. We talked about how to avoid being pulled into the office gossip. We discussed ways we could help the business. We discussed how to respond to the beggars and panhandlers on the streets.

My colleagues and I wore suits and silk ties to work. We felt uncomfortable walking past people who were sitting on the streets holding signs asking for change so they could eat, so our little group decided to do something. First, some of us decided to invite street people to our home for dinner so we could learn their stories. Second, we made an agreement with the management company that operated the underground parking lot below our office building. They gave us permission to offer a one-day job sweeping the parking area to any person we invited. However, we had to pay their wages. We began to offer such jobs but very few accepted them. For those who did, we were committed to finding other ways to help. We made it known to the other staff in the office so that they could make the same offer. This ended up stimulating an in-house company discussion on poverty and how we as a company might get involved with the poor and marginalized in our city.

Questions for Reflection:

1. In light of the "one another" commands in the Bible, why is teaming up important?
2. What is your personal experience with team work? What made it good (or not)?
3. Are you currently teamed up with other followers of Jesus at work? Why or why not?
4. A team consists of people who are committed to work together to achieve shared goals. What shared goals might motivate followers of Jesus at your workplace (or occupational sector) to form teams?
5. What might the agenda of a 60-minute weekly meeting for followers of Jesus at your workplace look like? Does it reflect the shared goals mentioned above?

Chapter 10

Increasing the Prominence of Our Priestly Identity

If you are acquainted with Hans Christian Andersen's fairy tale, The Ugly Duckling, then you are already familiar with the concept behind the term *reflected appraisal*. This is an academic term that

refers to the idea that our self-identity is shaped or misshaped by the appraisal/opinion of those in our social network.   As you may remember, the ugly duckling was actually a young swan who was hatched by ducks and raised as a duck. Because his stepparents, step siblings, and the other animals in the barn assumed he was a duck, he too assumed himself to be a duck although he was really a swan. It was not until he matured and met adult swans that he discovered his true identity. Knowing his true identity helped him make sense of his past. It also helped him set the direction for his future.

How about you? Has your true identity been obscured by reflected appraisals of those in your social circles? It has for most of us. The extent of other people's impact on our self-identity is influenced by many factors, not least of which is the appraiser's perceived credibility and the appraisal's consistency with our own beliefs about ourselves. Like the ugly duckling, many of us have been raised in a barn (metaphorically speaking), in that our priestly nature has never been acknowledged, reinforced, or nurtured. No wonder it is hard to embrace our priestly identity. But we can change that. It is not too late.

Taking Practical Action

The previous pages have focused on knowing and understanding our responsibility as priests. It is a good start, but not enough. To experience real change in increasing the prominence of our priestly identity, most of us will need continual reinforcement over a long period of time. Let me offer three suggestions:

1. First, become convinced in your own heart that *God* has made you a priest. For many of us, the idea that God has elevated us to such an important and honorable role is almost too much to take in. Our past experiences or present circumstances may seem to contradict the reality of our God-given priestly identity. We need to have our mind renewed (Romans 12:2) and that normally is a process that takes place over time as we learn and put into practice the teachings of Jesus. Fortunately Jesus is eager and able to help us. Some people protest, 'Not even Jesus can make a silk purse from a sow's ear.' I don't

know about that, but Jesus isn't primarily in the business of making silk purses from pigs' ears but in the business of cleaning, restoring, and repurposing damaged silk. I have found that prayer, mediation on Scripture, and earnest counsel with godly people is a crucial part of the renewal process. I have also found that our effectiveness as priests is less affected by where we are in the process than it is by our persevering in the process. We need to be committed to a life-long process of personal renewal.

2. Teaming up with others who want to live out their priestly identity is perhaps one of the most important single action you can do while working on point number one. We need to find others who are like-minded and willing to encourage and equip us in priestly attitudes and behaviors. When others see us as a priest, it helps us see ourselves as priests. Ideally our local church/fellowship provides this environment; but if not take the initiative to make it happen. We should keep an eye out for people to team up with in our workplace and professional sector. If you are unemployed or retired or do not have a workplace you can still team up with others. In whatever context you find yourself be proactive in praying, reconciling, inviting, encouraging, serving, and teaming up with others. Going about it alone is not how God designed it.

3. Encourage your local church. If you are a pastor, elder, or church leader, you can do much to promote and encourage the prominence of the congregation's priestly identity. For example you could:

   a. Constantly promote the importance and sanctity of all types of work.

   b. Each Sunday, have a different occupational group (e.g. nurses, teachers, public servants, etc.) stand up or be brought up front to be prayed over.

   c. Identify, facilitate, and honor fruitful workplace priests in your congregation.

   d. Officially appoint mentors and coaches from within the congregation.

   e. Regularly include testimonies of workplace stories at church meetings.

   f. Host weekly morning prayers for workplace priests (e.g. teaming up).

   g. Host communities of practice (teaming up by vocation).

   h. Expect the same activities from church members that you expect from your overseas missionaries.

   i. Honor workplace priests the same way overseas missionaries are honored.

   j. Host training events for people who are eager to embrace their role as workplace priests.

Summary

Our priestly nature is core to who we have become in Christ. It is part of our new nature[37] no matter what our ethnicity, spiritual gifts, talents, context, education, or vocation. We are priests, like it or not. Therefore, we need to embrace this identity by developing a lifestyle of priestly thinking and behaviors, especially at the workplace, where we spend so much of our time.

The six priestly behaviors of the P.R.I.E.S.T model (Praise, Reconcile, Invite, Encourage, Serve and Team-up) represent both attitudes and actions that are fundamental to our priestly nature. God bestowed us with dignity by making us his children, his servants, his saints, his friends, his disciples, and his ambassadors; all different facets of being his priests. Our priestly identity is designed to be expressed in unison with others, not just individually. Therefore, teaming up with others is fundamental to sustainability and fruitfulness.

---

[37] 2 Corinthians 5:17

Questions for Reflection:

1. On a scale of 0-10, how important do you believe it is to have a priestly self-identity at work? Why?
2. On a scale of 0-10, how prominent is your priestly self-identity?
3. Do you want that to increase? Why or why not?
4. What can you do to increase the prominence of your priestly self-identity?
5. What can you do to help others increase the prominence of their priestly self-identity?

References

Bash, A., Ambassadors for Christ: An Exploration of Ambassadorial Language in the New Testament, Tubingen, JCB Mohr, 1997.

Breslin, S., Church Planting Tracking and Analysis Tool, EMQ, pgs 508-515. October 2007, Wheaton, IL

Breslin, S and Jones, M., Understanding Dreams from God, William Carey Library Publishers, Pasadena, CA. 2004.

Burke, P.J. and Stets, J.E., Identity Theory, New York, Oxford University Press, 2009.

Dana, Daniel, Conflict Resolution, , McGraw-Hill, NY, 2001.

Guder, D.L., Missional Church: A Vision for the Sending of the Church in North America, Eerdmans Publishing, Grand Rapids, MI. 1998.

Love, R., Peace Catalysts: Resolving Conflict in Our Families, Organizations and Communities, InterVarsity Press, 2014.

Love, R., (2011) Following Jesus in a Glocalized World. Accessed 12 January 2015. http://ricklove.net/wp-content/uploads/2011/03/Following-Jesus-in-a-Glocalized-World-Rick-Love-2.pdf

Love, R., Peacemaking: Resoling Conflict, Restoring and Building Harmony Relationships, Pasadena, CA, William Carey Library. 2001.

McCall, G. J. and Simmons, J. L., Identities and interactions, New York, Free Press, 1978.

Root, J. and Guthire, S., The Sacrament of Evangelism, Chicago Il, Moody Press. 2001.

Scott, R., Evangelism and Dreams, Foundational Presuppositions to Interpret God-given Dreams of the Unreached, EMQ pages 176-184, April 2008, Wheaton, IL.

Stryker, S., Symbolic interactionism: A social structural version, Caldwell, New Jersey, Blackburn Press. 1980.

Sande, K., The Peacemaker: A Biblical Guide to Resolving Personal Conflict, Grand Rapids, Baker Book House. 1992.

Winter, S.F., Ambassadors for Christ: Ministry in the New Creation, in Anthony R. Cross and Ruth Gouldbourne (eds.), Questions of Identity: Studies in Honour of Brian Haymes, Centre for Baptist History and Heritage Studies 6; Oxford: Regent's Park College, 34–49, 2011

Personal notes:

Personal notes:

64122211R00051

Made in the USA
Middletown, DE
09 February 2018